Top 5 Business Lessons From
The Presidential Campaign
Of A Businessman

DONALD TRUMP

The Art Of Getting Attention

EF EntrepreneurshipFacts.com

Warning-Disclaimer!

The purpose of this book is to educate and entertain. The author or publisher does not guarantee that anyone following the techniques, suggestions, tips, ideas, or strategies will become successful. The author and publisher shall have neither liability or responsibility to anyone with respect to any loss or damage caused or alleged to be caused, directly or indirectly by the information contained in this book.

All information contained within this book has been researched from reputable sources. If any information is found to be false, please contact the publisher, who will be happy to make corrections for future editions.

Follow EntrepreneurshipFacts on social media to stay updated with our free book promotions and increase your knowledge about business and successful people on a daily basis:

Instagram Facebook Twitter

Also check out our website for the latest facts and articles about business and entrepreneurship:

www.EntrepreneurshipFacts.com

TABLE OF CONTENTS

Introduction: 6
Donald Trump – The Man 8
Strategy #1 – Get Attention at All Costs! 14
   Be Noticeable! 14
   Create Messaging That Incites a Reaction 16
   Define the Brands of Your Rivals 18
   Take a Stand 20
   Spin Controversy! 23
Strategy #2 – Know All the Players in the Game . 27
   Media 28
   Competition 34
   Target Market 38
   Raving Fans 40
   Non-Supporters or "Haters" 44
Strategy #3 – Keep an Authentic and Consistent Brand! 49
   The Authentic Trump Attitude 55
   The Authentic Trump Style 58
   The Authentic Trump "Diplomacy" 62
   Authenticity Builds Relationships 65
Strategy #4 – Adopt a Clear and Simple Mission Statement 69
   Choose the Wording Carefully 69
   Focus on Being Inclusive 75
Strategy #5 – Dominate Social Media! 78
   Departure from Television Advertising 80
   Twitter Marketing 83

Facebook and Internet Marketing 85
Promotional Products 89
Consistency and the Personal Touch through Digital Communications 90

Conclusion 92
10 Most Outrageous Donald Trump Quotes 96

Introduction:

Regardless of your place on the political spectrum, it's hard to deny the marketing prowess Donald Trump has exhibited throughout the course of his political campaign. Using the background and expertise he garnered in the marketing world, Trump has strategically applied this knowledge to bolster his political success in running for President of the United States.

Trump's tactics have captured the world's attention as they watch a business mogul take on the political arena, and his unconventional approach has undeniably changed both the political landscape and the expectations of the voting public. Throughout the course of his campaign, the strategies Donald Trump has exhibited offer an interesting perspective in how long-standing business and marketing strategies can transition perfectly into a different context, namely the political realm.

This book will delve into the primary marketing strategies Trump has employed in driving his campaign forward, and explore why these strategies have been successful, specifically focusing on *Getting Attention at All Costs, Knowing All the Players in the Game, Keeping an Authentic and Consistent Brand, Dominating Social Media*, and *Adopting a Clear and Simple Mission Statement*.

> *"[Trump's campaign] is such a very interesting marketing story and fascinating to watch from that lens. Politics is always about positions, but at its core, about marketing."*
> *~ Tim Calkins, Kellogg School of Management*

Donald Trump – The Man

Donald John Trump was born June 14, 1946 to Fred and Mary Trump in Queens, New York. As a successful real estate developer and builder in the city, it made perfect sense that Fred's son would follow in his footsteps.

As a confident, ambitious and energetic child, his parents sent him to the New York Military Academy at the young age of 13, where he would thrive as a successful and popular student. Graduating in 1964, Donald was recognized for his stellar academic record, strong athletic performance and had a reputation among his peers as a student leader. He started his secondary education at Fordham University, later transferring to the esteemed Wharton School of Finance, where he obtained a degree in economics.

Donald Trump may have appeared to follow in his father's footsteps, entering the world of real estate development; but he also had a competitive and ambitious drive for more that pushed him even further. Working alongside his father on weekends and over summer holidays, he quickly learned the ropes and absorbed as much as he could about running a business. Moving on to a fulltime position at his father's company, Elizabeth Trump & Son, he oversaw a variety of rental apartments in the greater New York area. Donald relentlessly pushed his father to expand the business by taking out loans on the apartments, and by 1971, had taken over the family business and renamed it to The Trump Organization.

With Donald Trump in charge, the Trump Organization soon set its sights on the economic potential of Manhattan, and began to get involved with a number of large development projects in the area. Not only did these projects generate impressive revenue, but they also solidified his brand and carved out Trump's reputation for upscale architecture and strong business acumen. As he acquired additional real estate and built a number of properties, his reputation as an astute businessman flourished. The development of the Commodore, a Penn Central Hotel, along with the Grand Hyatt Hotel in 1980, earned Trump an unparalleled reputation as one of New York's most successful and acclaimed real estate developers.

Over the following 35 years, Trump's real estate holdings, commercial developments and startups saw continued expansion. His countless ventures included Trump Tower, Trump Plaza Hotel and Casino, Trump's Castle in Atlantic City, The Trump Taj Mahal (this went bankrupt and was closed in 2016), Trump Parc, Television City, along with several skyscrapers and a park on the riverfront. Bolstering his thriving reputation for real estate, Trump entered the television world in 2004, becoming the start of NBC's *The Apprentice*. By all accounts, the show was highly successful, generating a large following and resulting in a number of spin-offs, including *The Celebrity Apprentice*. Following Trump's successful entry into the television world, he collaborated with NBC to produce the Miss USA and Miss Universe Pageants, a relationship that would collapse in 2015 after Trump's inappropriate comments about minorities and immigration.

Trump's private life was more tumultuous; his first marriage was to fashion model Ivana Winklmayr, with whom he had three children: Donald Trump, Jr.; Ivanka Trump and Eric Trump. Following a nasty and public divorce in 1991, Trump married again in 1993, this time to an actress. After the birth of another child, Tiffany, the couple divorced in 1997. In 2005, Trump married model Melania Knauss, with whom he had another child, Barron Trump, in 2006.

Since the 1988 presidential election, Trump has been considered a potential candidate for President in nearly every election. However, he was never serious about it until the 2016 election. Donald Trump formally announced his candidacy on June 16, 2015, with a campaign rally and speech at Trump Tower in New York City. He declared that he would self-fund his presidential campaign, and would refuse any money from donors and lobbyists. With seemingly no real previous political aspirations or experience, he transitioned his expertise from the business world to carve out a new niche in the political arena.

Strategy #1 – Get Attention at All Costs!

Be Noticeable!

As any marketer knows well, to be successful, a brand must first get noticed; and this has been an area where Trump has undoubtedly excelled. Gaining attention for your brand or product is paramount, and in the political arena, getting attention from voters is no different. Donald Trump has garnered an incredible amount of attention by putting this strategy into action. Regardless of their political viewpoints, his candidacy has truly captured the world's attention.

> *"Love him or hate him, we all know about Donald Trump's presidential campaign. We hear about and see it every day. In fact, it's one of the most relevant and*

frequently mentioned topics on media, period."
~ AJ Agrawal, Forbes Contributor

Getting attention, even negative attention, is key in solidifying a strong reputation. Age-old marketing principles state that generating an interest about your offer is the first step to creating leads, which ultimately turn into sales. Applying the same principles within the political arena, creating a draw and capturing attention is propelling Trump's success. With a society that has grown disillusioned with the same speeches, promises and statistics they have become accustomed to hearing, Trump has perfected the art of getting attention, no matter what the cost.

Create Messaging That Incites a Reaction

One of Trump's most noticeable strategies is to make statements that incite emotion and demand attention. While these statements may be unexpected, outlandish or controversial, they have been incredibly effective in capturing the attention of his target market, otherwise known as voters. During speeches, debates, press conferences, television interviews, or even face-to-face conversations, Trump seems to always take advantage of the opportunity to say something that demands the attention of his audience. Time and time again, he is undeniably able to garner attention and keep the conversation centered on his campaign. While some may argue he has attracted a significant amount of negative press, it is attention nonetheless; and consequently, Trump has accomplished a marketer's dream: to get people talking.

Theoretically, marketing experts are unlikely to advocate for politically incorrect or offensive statements as a means to garner attention for their brand. However, Trump has repeatedly employed this strategy to get others to pay attention. From fans and supporters to his fiercest rivals, people continue to watch, to listen, and to engage with his messages. Regardless of why Trump has such a captive audience, the business world, especially marketing professionals, deeply understand how important awareness is to any brand's success.

Define the Brands of Your Rivals

Donald Trump has consistently employed an intriguing tactic to get attention on the campaign trail – bestowing his rivals with specific nicknames, ranging from "Crooked Hillary" and "Lyin' Ted" to "Little Marco" and "Crazy Bernie." While this may be thought of as underhanded, it is serving to get attention and simultaneously devalue and undermine his rivals. In most cases, this strategy wouldn't be effective, as many individuals would consider this to be defamation, or an indication of immaturity at least. However, interestingly enough, Trump has used this tactic repeatedly to benefit his candidacy. While it may be a polarizing tactic, it has undeniably helped earn him the presidential nomination as the Republican Party's candidate.

For the average person, it may be difficult to recall any such nicknames that have been affiliated with

Trump. The reason nothing comes to mind is because his political rivals haven't employed the same tactics. While Trump may be occasionally labeled with a nickname, its staying power is negligible. Meanwhile, Trump has been hugely successful in "branding" his political rivals by not only creating these affiliations and instigating character judgments, but also succeeded in reinforcing their brand by repeating these names on a regular basis. In what seems to be an effective tactic borrowed from the playbook of a savvy marketer, Trump's consistent messaging is essentially helping to shape the image of his political rivals.

Take a Stand

The next marketing strategy that Trump employs depicting a specific stance on issues that is both unique and memorable. As those in the marketing world will attest, companies or individuals wanting to create a solid brand shouldn't be concerned about pushing away the people who don't align with them. In any marketing situation, some individuals will always respond negatively to your messaging or reject your brand, but that is fine--they're simply not your target market. Rather than focusing on these people, marketers are urged to take a stand that draws attention and attracts a loyal and enthusiastic audience. Consider the presidential candidates through the lens of an average citizen who listens to mainstream news, watches the occasional debate or takes in the odd political paper. Regardless of political viewpoint, it's difficult to think of any specific and surprisingly memorable policies or plans the Democratic Party or Hillary Clinton have unveiled. Their stance about better gun laws or immigrants gaining citizenship may come to mind, but Clinton especially hasn't honed in on key topics with the same focus and fixation that Trump has.

One the other hand, Trump has made a countless number of controversial but memorable promises and plans for change. While many individuals may be opposed to his suggested policies, they will undeniably be able to reference several unforgettable promises he has made throughout the course of his political campaign. His promise to build a wall between Mexico and the United States, ensuring that Mexico bears the cost; a temporary restriction on Muslims traveling to America; or the use of waterboarding and other torture tactics in the war on terrorism. In each case, these controversial and provocative topics have incited an emotional reaction from voters and left a memorable imprint in the minds of the public.

Regardless of an individual's political viewpoint, it is indisputable that Trump has consistently employed provocative words and descriptions to ensure his messages are unforgettable to both his supporters and rivals. Consequently, his marketing and political strategies have served to ensure he is consistently getting noticed--and this tactic has been undoubtedly successful. His plans are being noticed and his policies talked about. Whether they are strong supporters or the most bitter of adversaries, people are continuing to engage. This is what marketers call brand recognition.

> *"[Trump] says things that are forbidden, and he isn't apologetic about it. He comes across as a complicated and flawed but authentic person. People forgive the content because they vicariously experience the seemingly unscripted spontaneity behind it."*
> *~ Michael Bader, AlterNet*

Spin Controversy!

Controversy has undoubtedly arisen from some of the strategies Trump has chosen to employ. In marketing, negative attention from extreme tactics such as these can be quite risky. By inciting a strong, negative reaction, adversaries can use this against your brand, and the target market--or in this case, voters--may begin to think negatively about the person in question. However, Donald Trump has consistently "spun" controversy to ensure his thoughts and viewpoints are perceived in a favorable way whenever possible.

One strong example is Trump's highly contentious messaging about banning Muslims, building a wall on the Mexico border, and deporting illegal immigrants. While these provocative viewpoints generated a host of accusations that he is xenophobic (having an intense and irrational fear of people from other countries), Trump spun the messaging and dismissed the criticism by reminding voters that his wives have come from other countries and he has developed strong professional relationships with foreigners through his various international businesses.

Another conflict that came up between Trump and Hillary Clinton, his main adversary, was medical records. Mainstream media reported that Trump's doctor was pressured into declaring him fit for the presidency. Countering this message, Trump unexpectedly challenged Clinton, stating he was more than willing to make detailed medical records available to the public if she would commit to do the same. In this case, Trump was employing a strategic public relations tactic to deflect attention and put the adversary on the defensive. Employing his experience and insight from the business world, Trump perfectly transitioned his knowledge to apply to the political realm. By invalidating or downplaying criticism, an individual can force the opposition into a defensive role by countering criticism and returning even greater accusations.

In the early days of Trump's campaign, there was significant controversy pertaining to a few of Trump's failed businesses. Claiming to be an instinctive and financially smart business leader, he faced criticism from his adversaries who demanded to know why a number of his businesses had gone bankrupt. Trump quickly explained that this was simply a matter of numbers; while it couldn't be denied that a few of his businesses had failed, he had been wildly successful in countless other ventures. While he never denied these bankruptcies had taken place, he changed the narrative to craft an inspiring story of overcoming setbacks and coming out even better on the other side. This strategy of spinning negative attention and controversy has been executed many times throughout his political campaign. By spinning messages, Trump has not only countered some of the criticism he's received, but has also seemed to be successful and changing these messages to actually reinforce his qualifications and position him in a better light.

Strategy #2 – Know All the Players in the Game!

> *"One of the key problems today is that politics is such a disgrace, good people don't go into government."*
> *~ Donald Trump*

Since his background as a business mogul right through his transition into the political world, Donald Trump has made it a point to know everyone in the game. A valuable marketing strategy, this served him well in both business and politics. In the "game" of politics, it is undeniable that Trump has been a strong contender. In the marketing realm, having a deep knowledge of all competitors is key to ensuring your offer is strong and your approach is strategic. In the political game Trump now finds himself immersed in, some of the other stakeholders would be the media, his competition or rivals, his target market, raving fans, and his non-supporters.

Media

The media plays a huge role in Mr. Trump's campaign marketing strategies, and he seems to intentionally create conflict in order to garner their attention. Put simply, Trump is well aware that attention from the media is vital to his success. As the main source of information to the general public, his ability to engage with the media is essential to getting his messages shared effectively. To anyone who regularly reads the news or watches television, it is evident that the media has often had a contentious relationship with Trump. Meanwhile, Trump seems very attuned to the fact that he is inciting controversy and uses this to fuel and support his political campaign.

While his dissentious platform may inspire the wrath of many, Donald Trump has been able to market his brand with the media so well, he has essentially received around $3 billion worth of advertising at no cost due to the strategies employs with the media. With Trump's high net worth in mind, it seems ironic that he may very well have the means to pay out of pocket for advertising costs, yet likely receives more free advertising than any other candidate due to these tactics.

As the presidential candidate with arguably the *least* support from mainstream media outlets, it becomes evident that Trump's experience in the business world has greatly benefitted his political run. For the most part, America's main television networks are thought of as more supportive of his primary rival's ideology and campaign. However, because Trump is skilled at garnering attention, the media consistently provides him with airtime due to popular demand; ranging from his ardent supporters to his bitter adversaries, the public is always interested in hearing the latest controversial musings of Donald Trump. While this tactic may result in significant backlash, it can also be thought of as a brilliant marketing strategy, with an individual ultimately manipulating their adversary into creating more publicity for the brand.

One of Trump's most noticeable traits has been his refusal to "play by the rules" that other politicians have complied with for decades. His provocative demeanor with reporters throughout countless press conferences adds a sense of excitement that other candidates have not been able to generate. The media themselves seem to be at a loss as to whether Trump will actually answer questions, *how* he will answer them, which reporters he may insult, which ones he will refuse to interact with, and exactly what he may say. While the media may be frustrated by his deflection of questions and occasional refusal to answer, they also know the characteristics the public have began to expect from Trump create demand, evoke a response and increase viewership. Because Trump's strategies for getting attention work so well, the media can be confident they will always have a "story" to share after each interaction.

> *"The rise of Trump has created a great debate within the media on how to cover him. In the competition for viewers and web traffic that help media outlets make money, Trump coverage makes sense. And by a number of measures, the public is deeply interested in Trump."*
> *~ Perry Bacon, Jr., NBC News*

Another situation that presented itself was that between Trump and Meghan Kelly, a Fox reporter and debate moderator. After moderating a debate for Republican candidates, Kelly was subject to the wrath of Donald Trump following one particular debate. With an aversion to her style of moderating and strong dislike of the questions she asked, Trump refused to be involved with Kelly in the future. Going forward, Trump would decline any invitation where Kelly was the moderator, and the media soon realized that Trump would only attend an event after confirming that Kelly would not be part of it. Even after Trump received the Republican Party's nomination for President, he employed a similar tactic. Rather than jumping into opportunities to debate his opponents, he appeared to cautiously screen invitations in order to prepare for which moderators would be participating and ensure that he would be positioned favorably.

Trump has continuously employed a classic marketing tactic; regardless of how the media may feel about him, what he stands for, his policies, or his personality, they are inadvertently drawn in by his polarizing behavior and controversial messages. Trump seems to truly *know* the media; from manipulating them into providing free advertising or simply giving him a sounding board, "knowing the players" has been an exceptionally valuable tactic in Trump's campaign.

Competition

Donald Trump has successfully utilized the age-old marketing strategy of knowing the competition and taken it to a whole new level throughout the course of his political campaign. Whether he is competing for the job of President of the United States against fellow Republicans or the Democratic opposition, Trump has continuously demonstrated how well he knows who they are, what they stand for, and how to incite a reaction. This knowledge has equipped him with the information needed to counter their criticism and respond appropriately, and it has also given him a pathway to differentiate himself from the competition. As those in the marketing world will attest, a company can easily be outmaneuvered, outplayed, and eventually put out of business if it do not know its adversaries well enough to compete with them strategically.

> *"My father always said, 'Know everything you can about what you're doing'."*
> *~ Donald Trump*

The fact that the economy was booming in the 1990s during Bill Clinton's presidency is thought of as one of the main strengths of Hillary Clinton's campaign. While Trump cannot deny the fact that the economy flourished during Bill Clinton's time, he attributes part of the reason for the current state of the economy to the NAFTA signed by Clinton during his presidency. While the accuracy of this allegation may be disputable, it creates a cloud of doubt around a topic that would otherwise propel Clinton forward, and also shifts the focus away from Trump's lack of experience in politics.

Trump's knowledge about the competition could be considered even more valuable in his hands than in the hands of an average politician, as he seems unafraid to use this knowledge as leverage, regardless of the consequences. Trump's competition has used his multiple marriages and divorces as evidence of an underlying attitude towards women. However, his primary rival Hillary Clinton, along with her husband, have faced their own scandals in the past as well. Bill Clinton's affairs, and Hillary's reaction, have long served as fodder for scandalous headlines both during and after Bill Clinton's rein as President. Honing in on these weaknesses in their campaign and consistently referencing the situation throughout his own campaign has been effective in undermining any success they may have had in criticizing Trump's marital issues.

The clearest example of how important it is to know your competition was evident in how Donald Trump successfully outplayed his rival, Ted Cruz, during the primaries. In the early days of Trump's campaign, Cruz seemed not only to be keeping pace with Trump in the polls, but at times pulling ahead of him. However, by exploiting an issue in Cruz' personal life, Cruz' effectiveness as a leader was called into question. After witnessing such a defensive and passionate response from Cruz, Trump knew he had successfully evoked the response he wanted and was ultimately successful in stifling Cruz' campaign momentum. In the past, the immediate families of politicians have been thought of as "off limits" for criticism, but similar to many times before, Donald Trump refused to play by the traditional "rules" and was rewarded by his eventual win over Cruz. While some may criticize this as an unethical tactic, it was undoubtedly successful in moving him forward.

Target Market

As marketers are well aware, understanding your target market is of utmost importance. Donald Trump seems to have honed in on the audiences that support him, and worked hard to attract their attention in a meaningful way. While he may offend various segments of the population with his controversial messaging, he also focuses on main points that are top priorities for a majority of the public. Trump's proposals for solving nationwide problems are often controversial or antagonistic towards minority groups, but by focusing on critical issues and addressing them continuously, he has fallen in favor with a large group of people. Some of Trump's primary messages include the state of the economy, American safety, addressing terrorism, problems with the healthcare system, and the corruption of the political system as a whole. Regardless of one's political stance or position, these are all issues that strongly resonate with the general public. A successful marketing strategy involves understanding your target market well enough to effectively address their pain points, and Trump has undoubtedly been successful in executing this strategy.

> *"Trump knows how to work an audience. He knows what people want, and he knows how to give it to them. Trump is a sales person at heart, and he knows how to win people over."*
> *~ AJ Agrawal, Forbes Contributor*

Raving Fans

As business marketers know well, it is important to retain customers and inspire a strong sense of brand loyalty if you want to achieve long-term success. After all, those who believe in a business and its products are not only likely to be repeat customers, but they can also serve as ambassadors for your brand and generate new customers. Throughout the course of his campaign, Donald Trump has demonstrated a clear understanding of exactly who supports him and his message, why they support him, and what he needs to do to win them over.

Our society has an insatiable appetite for information, but also wants information that is clear, easy to access and relevant. Trump demonstrates a deep understanding of this concept and has reacted by providing more information on social media than any other candidate before him. With a vast following on Facebook, Twitter, and other social networks, Trump has consistently connected with his supporters through social media.

Trump also demonstrates the ability to hone in on the deep fears of his supporters and confidently convey that he will work to fix these problems immediately should he become President. For example, he knows many of his supporters are disturbed by and deeply afraid of radical and extreme Islamic terrorists, so has consequently expressed his intent and solutions for "Making America Safe Again." He knows how frustrated many of his supporters are with their perception of politicians having deep ties in the politics scene, and consequently looks for every opportunity to reinforce his position as an "outsider" who isn't afraid to be different. Leveraging his supporters' beliefs about governmental corruption, Trump repeatedly reaffirms that he is not part of "the system". By reiterating his inability to be bribed or corrupted by the agenda of any political party, he is speaking directly to his supporters who see him as an adversary of the status quo. Supporters who are frustrated with other parties making backroom deals or securing alliances to further their own agendas feel at ease when Trump claims he is an outsider to the corrupt political world.

> *"The problems we face now – poverty and violence at home, war and destruction abroad – will last only as long as we continue relying on the same politicians who created them in the first place."*
> *~ Donald Trump*

Utilizing his business acumen and experience, Donald Trump seemed to realize early in his campaign that the movers and shakers of the younger generations (Millennials and Generation Z) place significant value on authenticity – much more than any other generation has before. By employing this marketing tactic, Trump has continued to reinforce his own authenticity. Regardless of political viewpoint, Trump's brand is consistently Trump. His fans and adversaries alike can expect to hear his true thoughts on a subject, giving no thought to "political correctness" or worry about offending someone. In an era of countless scandals and secrecy uncovered throughout the ranks of politician among all parties, Trump's brand of authenticity may be one of the most-effective marketing strategies he has used.

Non-Supporters or "Haters"

The best marketers comprehend the value of their non-supporters, or "haters" and capitalize on the benefits they can bring to marketing campaign strategies. Valuable in the marketing world, Donald Trump seems to understand that the political arena is no different. Trump's strategic utilization of those who don't support him only serves to demonstrate his marketing expertise. In the business world, non-supporters can be an incredible asset or a detriment to success – depending on how they are approached and how they are managed. Being in the unusual position of being involved in both the business and political world, Trump has demonstrated his expertise at managing these people throughout the election process and using them to propel his brand forward.

In the marketing world, how people are advised to deal with "haters" depends on the situation and the type of business. Some marketing experts will recommend that these people be ignored completely rather than wasting time, energy, and money trying to counter their criticism. Other times, experts encourage business owners to speak up and defend their brand in order to improve their public image. Trump utilizes both tactics, but he rarely ignores these people for long.

In order to inspire confidence in your brand, you must eventually address issues or points that are being criticized by your adversaries. As a business, demonstrating confidence and defending your brand shows people that what you are being criticized for is not always valid, and what you are offering is valuable enough to defend. While Trump has defended his political brand ferociously, he has learned to express it in a way that conveys his apathy to those who are criticizing him. Rather than becoming emotional, he defends his calmly or at least in a way that aligns with his usual demeanor.

> *"There's nothing better than showing the world...that you'll stand up for your company and defend your brand."*
> *~ Adam Callinan*

The number of haters Trump continuously attracts and the intensity of their criticism is a factor Trump has used to his advantage. Rarely ignoring criticism from his rivals for long, he speaks up to defend his brand and his position in politics quite frequently. In fact, Trump uses those who criticize him to actually bolster his support and strengthen the resolve of his voters. His business sense has allowed him to recognize the value of these adversaries and not shy away from them as other politicians may have the tendency to do. Consequently, when his words and actions invoke the wrath of his adversaries, it often results in his most ardent supporters jumping in to defend him. The more emotional and angry people become, the easier it becomes to defend against them. Reminiscent of the business rivalry between Apple and Samsung, the fans of the brand will jump to its defense, and the company can simply stand by and watch the process unfold.

> *"When this is done effectively, other onlookers get involved in the defense of your position – which often creates a sense of community, and even [attracts] new customers that may not have been previously interested in your product."*
> *~ Adam Callinan*

Not only do Trump's critics provide a unique platform for his supporters to defend him from, they also continue to ensure that attention is focused on Trump's messages, rather than the other candidates. Instead of voters focusing on the positive messages of the candidate they support, setting their sights on the opposition actually results in attention being focuses squarely on Trump's campaign. While Trump's adversaries attempt to draw attention to the flaws and inconsistencies of his campaign, their efforts effectively move Clinton's campaign out of the limelight. As Trump learned long ago in the business arena, when approached effectively, the criticism received by a company's adversaries can actually boost its brand, while silencing a competing brand.

Strategy #3 – Keep an Authentic and Consistent Brand!

Before Donald Trump had carved out a reputation in the political world, he was a big name with an even bigger presence in the business world. Well known around the world for decades, the Trump quite literally built an empire and fortune centered around one single word – Trump. The "Trump" brand became synonymous with the man: opulent, grand, brash, and powerful. Throughout the real estate, architecture or even television industries, Trump created an impressive brand that immediately conveys who he is, what he represents, and a host of connotations upon hearing his name. Across a wide range of sectors and circumstances, Trump's brand evokes an unprecedented spirit of confidence, authenticity and power.

In this day and age of "scripted" personalities and disconnection between perception and reality, Trump is seen by many as refreshingly authentic and consistently true to who he is. While some may react negatively to his viewpoints or campaign, there is a noticeable lack of surprising revelations or "secrets" about his personal life or his brand. Building a legacy for himself by capitalizing on his own sense of authenticity, he has employed one of the most valuable marketing tools possible.

> *"All the presidential candidates are seeking to build their" brand" and create one that people will support because they believe it's in their self-interest. Trump has managed to do exactly what great brands need to do."*
> *~ James Warren, Forbes Contributor*

Trump's campaign manager, Corey Lewandowski, had a simple strategy. In the early stages of his campaign, Lewandowski wrote four powerful words across a whiteboard during a planning session: "Let Trump be Trump." This strategy would prove to be as valuable in crafting his brand in the political arena as it was in the business world. Regardless of their political viewpoint, those who know Trump seem to be confident that they understand what he's all about. While his authenticity might not have garnered him much political support in earlier decades, today's younger generations are all about authenticity. For consumers, authenticity is more important than ever before for those making purchasing decisions, which marketers have started to realize. Consumers across all sectors are increasingly demanding more transparency from their favorite brands, and by conveying a sense of authenticity, Trump has undoubtedly been able to achieve a strong political edge against his rivals.

When it comes to marketing, consumers are increasingly turned off by clever messages and underhanded manipulation tactics, and the political world is no different. Canned speeches, pre-written scripts, and candidates who say exactly what is expected are perceived more negatively than in the past. Now, society is looking for someone who they believe remains true to who they are – even if that includes a bit of negative press. One of the most consistently repeated claims about Trump is that "he says what he thinks," whether that is politically correct or not. While this can also be a detriment to his brand, it has served him well considering the current political climate. Donald Trump's success clearly demonstrates that regardless of whether appearances reflect reality, being perceived as authentic is of utmost importance to a brand, product, or politician.

> *"Authenticity just requires that a person says what she believes, not that she says what is true."*
> ~ Mike LaBossiere, Talking Philosophy

Whether consumers, clients or voters, people have a desire to support something they believe to be truly authentic. Nobody wants to feel as though they have been misled or manipulated into believing something, only to discover so later. Throughout the course of his political campaign, Trump has utilized strategies that indicate a deep understanding of this concept. Continuously, Trump reinforces his own authenticity or attempts to discredit his opponent's authenticity, and both tactics have generated credibility for his campaign.

Even his strongest adversaries seem to appreciate his "realness" and his unfiltered, straightforward style. The Trump brand is raw and unapologetic. As marketers know well, ensuring the brand message and tone stays true to the product or service being sold is absolutely essential. When potential customers can believe in what the brand is portraying, they are much more willing to overlook imperfections or issues and have more confidence about the brand itself.

The Authentic Trump Attitude

There are a number of examples where Trump has been able to portray authenticity in the business world as well as in the political arena. Many people will note the similarities between Trump's business and political personas, ultimately because Trump doesn't appear to change much based on his environment. While there are always exceptions, Trump communicates his authenticity quite consistently – which is a powerful tool for any marketing campaign, business or political.

No Regrets

When thinking about Donald Trump, many people will remember his consistently unapologetic attitude. He rarely expresses a sense of regret over anything and tends to treat failure as simply a tool that provides experience and equips him for even greater success. His political opponents have tirelessly tried to negate his financial success and called attention to his tumultuous business history and multiple ventures that went bankrupt. With this record, his opponents have asked how he would manage the finances of the United States if he has been unsuccessful in managing his own companies. Trump has been able to counter these claims well simply by refusing to express any regret or shame about the failures. Instead, he has lauded the virtue of his failures as experiences that will serve to equip him for future success and actually turn around the negative economic state of the country. Rather than denying the bankruptcies, he has changed the narrative to position his failure as a positive attribute rather than apologizing for it.

> *"What separates the winners from the losers is how a person reacts to each new twist of fate."*
> *~ Donald Trump*

Manages Critics and Naysayers

By predominantly ignoring the critics and naysayers that he undeniably attracts, Trump has remained true to his brand. A consistent thread throughout his political campaign, Trump makes minimal attempts to placate critical voters or individuals who question his ability to lead the country. In the early stages of his run for the Republican nomination, huge numbers of people expressed amusement and disbelief that Trump would get anywhere in his bid for public office. Along with his inability to fit the political mold, Trump made no attempts to convince naysayers that he could be a "real" politician if they would give him a chance. Instead, he responded with an unwavering confidence that seemed to catch the world off guard. Likewise, a successful business doesn't beg consumers to believe in a product; rather, they exhibit an unwavering confidence in what is being offered and provide a way for potential buyers to support the product.

The Authentic Trump Style

Thinking about Donald Trump's fashion style and general appearance, his distinct hairstyle will often be the first thing to come to mind. It's not by accident that voters immediately connect that reddish-gold, fluffy hairstyle to Trump. While some may mock his unconventional style, professional marketers know that creating a strong and memorable presence is important. Brand recognition is a major factor in any successful campaign, and even within a political arena, Trump has come to realize that his presidential campaign will greatly benefit from a strong brand. While hairstyle may seem like a tiny detail, it again serves to reinforce his "authenticity" and provide tangible proof of the individuality he consistently flaunts. Regardless of the countless comments or endless jokes, his hairstyle tells others he refuses to change for anyone, adding further credibility to his brand of "authenticity".

> *"I get a lot of credit for comb-overs, but it's not really a comb-over. It's sort of a little bit forward and back. I've combed it the same way for years. Same thing. Every time."*
>
> *Donald Trump*

In marketing, brands are often advised not to fear showing a bit of weakness. Logically, people know that nothing is perfect, so demonstrating minor flaws can actually win the trust of your audience. Instead of raising suspicion that imperfections are being glossed over, a consumer is more likely to rank a brand as believable or authentic if they openly admit to the occasional stumbling point. Similarly, Trump may have benefited from this strategy due to his unconventional hairstyle. As politicians demonstrate they are human, voters and constituents are more likely to support them. Although countless jokes are made, Trump seems completely unbothered by those who make a mockery out of his hairstyle. Instead, he relishes the fact that talking about his hair is ultimately talking about him, which means he's getting attention and mind space from potential voters. While Trump employs this strategy, he is not the first; many successful and renowned politicians have had some type of feature or physical factor for which they are lightheartedly teased. Ultimately, this can work in the person's favor and subtly position them as a real and authentic person.

Well aware of everything his brand represents, Trump stays consistent. While he has received advice to scale back his controversial comments, tone down his personality or sugarcoat his provocative speeches to be more palatable for mainstream voters, he has consistently rejected this advice. Although many don't think highly of his political stance, policies or attitude, he has commanded a certain amount of respect simply by holding true to his brand and refusing to compromise.

The Authentic Trump "Diplomacy"

As many will attest, Donald Trump has never been described as politically correct. However, he has used his plain language and perceived lack of diplomacy as evidence of his sincerity. Countless voters have grown frustrated with carefully crafted speeches and scripted key messages that focus on not offending, rather than being realistic about the country's challenges. Using this knowledge, Trump has ensured his messages are always simple, straightforward and emotionally charged. Although his lack of sensitivity on topics such as terrorism or border control can be offensive to many people, others have "bought" what he's selling, finding him relatable and agreeing about the challenges that need to be faced. As a marketer must focus on addressing the pain point of their audience, Trump has come to realize that his target market, the voters, are searching for someone who can offer solutions without the perceived bureaucracy of crafting palatable, non-offensive messaging that doesn't get to the heart of an issue.

> *"I think the big problem this country has is being politically correct. I've been challenged by so many people, and I don't frankly have time for total political correctness. And to be honest with you, the country doesn't have time either."*
> *~ Donald Trump*

While this may be a fine line to walk in both the business and political world, it appears Trump has been able to successfully tap into the mindset of his supporters who are happy to see problems being acknowledged, even if messaging is being delivered via a blunt and abrasive speech. Trump's unfiltered approach has won over a significant amount of voters who have become frustrated with what they perceive as watered down, generic language designed to not offend. While historically, the public has appreciated the ability of politicians to talk in a polished, charming way, the current political climate seeks authenticity above all. Trump's disregard for being politically correct and refusal to fall into line has been a remarkably successful strategy in his campaign so far.

Authenticity Builds Relationships

Experienced marketers are well aware that great customers and potential supporters seek authenticity and consistency in order to believe in what they're being sold. While this concept is a given in the business world, Trump has demonstrated it can also serve as a marketing technique in the political arena as well. Any savvy marketer knows that in order to sell something, a personal connection must first be made; and connecting on a personal level requires a dose of authenticity. Authenticity is expressed when your principles and opinions are defined clearly and maintained unapologetically, even when challenged or criticized. While many people reject his viewpoints and opinions, he has won credibility as he stands firm in his beliefs in spite of the backlash he receives. As time goes on and his principles are consistently expressed despite endless pushback, he only seems to gain more credibility from his followers.

> *"Part of being authentic is a matter of not have certain qualities: not being scripted, not presenting an act, and not saying what one things the audience wants to hear."*
> *~ Mike LaBossiere, Talking Philosophy*

While Trump's expression of authenticity can be perceived as rude and abrasive, this approach is not without its benefits, as it allows him to stand out within a political arena. Although some may disagree with his comments, they seem to respect the fact that he is willing to speak his mind and accept any backlash that may result. Evidently, Trump judged the situation well initially; realizing his authentic and unfiltered style of communication was completely unique and something that would let him stand out in the political world. While other politicians may appear to waver as they speak strategically, shaping themselves to whatever their audience or the situation calls for, Donald Trump refuses to play this game. However, in the current political climate, this was a gamble that definitely paid off. By carving out this niche, Trump has been able to effectively market his disregard for the status quo and capitalize on being everything the other politicians are not.

Trump's portrayal of authenticity holds some lessons for many marketers. One of the most valuable selling points throughout his campaign is that he does not change. In or out of the White House, his supporters have confidence that they won't be signing up for the unexpected; many will say that while he may not use eloquent language and charming key messages, the fear of the unknown is worse for them than a reality that's a bit rough around the edges. It seems to be of little importance whether this authenticity is real, as long as it appears to be. In the marketing world, people are much more likely to purchase a product if they truly believe the seller is authentic and trustworthy.

Those who change the focus of their business on a regular basis end up creating doubt in the mind of their target audience. As Trump seems to be aware, the first step in marketing is for your audience to believe you are who you say you are, before they will even consider buying your product. Changing your target audience or the problems you are claiming to solve only makes your company seem flighty and unstable. For customers to have a true sense of loyalty, they need to be confident in who you are, and know this won't change even when faced with pushback.

Strategy #4 – Adopt a Clear and Simple Mission Statement

"Trump knows what he is doing ... his rhetoric is simple, dramatic, and repetitive."
~ Arun Gupta, In These Times

Choose the Wording Carefully

Savvy marketers know that the more complicated the message is they are trying to communicate, the less likely it will be understood and adopted by the customers you are trying to attract. Taking a page from the marketer's playbook, Donald Trump's campaign slogan works perfectly for promoting his agenda in the clearest and most easily understood way possible. In fact, his political campaign needed to reach an even wider group of people than the average company; his constituents come from different ages, cultures, education levels, income levels, business experience and health status, yet each one of them must be able to understand his message regardless of their background. "Make America Great Again" resonates with many and has gained significant traction among his supporters. Simple and straightforward, it doesn't require an explanation, translation or additional information. While the connotations of the phrase will be different to each person, it is easy to understand and inspires confidence among his supporters.

Knowing that a confusing mission statement can sabotage a marketer's success, Trump has crafted a slogan that simultaneously acknowledges current challenges, reminisces about good times, and offers hope for creating a better future. The statement doesn't have to explain everything, but the idea of returning to the prosperity of past generations offers an intriguing option for those who are currently struggling. While the competition has disagreed with multiple areas of his mission statement, it's difficult to criticize the goal to "Make America Great". While the candidates may all disagree on how to accomplish this, it is an admirable goal regardless of political stance.

In the marketing world, the solution a company is proposing may be complex, but the ultimate goal must still be straightforward, clear and make an impact. Voters naturally find themselves agreeing that yes, they want to make the country great again, and the underlying message Trump hopes to get across is that his energy and enthusiasm is needed to accomplish this goal.

"Make America Great Again" is the perfect slogan because it is easily understood, easy to agree with, and also offers a general statement that any of his more complicated political tactics can fall under. When discussing complex plans, policies or stances, Trump can attempt to justify his method by claiming it is part of this greater goal.

A clear and simple theme is vital to marketing success, regardless of what you are selling, and Trump has been successful in capitalizing on this marketing strategy to propel his political campaign forward.

> *"He's taken a simple, relatively singular set of policy notions and tied them to that one overall benefit. He puts it all together in a pitch that resonates with people."*
> *~ James Warren, US News*

Once a positive marketing theme has been established, it is much more difficult for the competition to argue with. Trump's adversaries can certainly contest the specific methods of accomplishing his goal, but it is extremely difficult to argue against a mission that appears to benefit everyone. By establishing this clear and straightforward mission early on the campaign trail, Trump was able to get an edge on his competition. His strategic "Make America Great Again" could have worked well for promoting any party, so securing this slogan early in the process was highly beneficial to a successful campaign. In the business world, speed and timing can make an incredible difference in garnering the much-needed support and loyalty to successfully sell your product.

From a marketing perspective, Trump clearly was able to get an edge on his competitors by establishing his mission statement and choosing one that was difficult for the competition to argue with. If a brand can develop a powerful, simple, and clear slogan that is either better than the competition's or publicized first, it is well on its way towards outcompeting rival companies. In the political arena, this strategy clearly paid off for Donald Trump, giving him a leg up on the competition. After all, every American would agree that it's a desirable goal to "Make America Great Again".

> *"The direction I will outline today will also return us to a timeless principle. My foreign policy will always put the interests of the American people and American security above all else. That will be the foundation of every decision that I will make."*
> *Donald Trump*

Translate this into business; the problem your product is solving must appeal to a large enough market in order to be successful. Just like voters from all sides can agree they want America to be great, your business will succeed by creating a brand that is needed or wanted by a wide range of consumers. If your product or service is useful or enjoyed by a large segment of the population, you are well positioned for success.

Focus on Being Inclusive

After initially establishing a believable and easily understood campaign slogan for his political brand, Trump has done well in consistently holding onto that mission statement unapologetically. Regardless of criticism, he has not wavered from the theme of making America great again. In an attempt to discredit the idea, his competition has purported that America is already great; however, this hasn't resonated with populations that are struggling. In business, focusing solely on the positives of a situation sabotages your sales pitch and either makes people doubt whether they really need what you are selling, or makes them think you don't truly understand the challenges they're facing.

> *"You know the funny thing, I don't get along with rich people. I get along with the middle class and the poor people better than I get along with the rich people."*
> *~ Donald Trump*

Trump's platform of making America great again seems to resonate with virtually every demographic, as it is general enough to encase all of the problems threatening the life, liberty, and happiness of Americans. In the business world, entrepreneurs strive to offer relevant products and solutions for whatever challenges their potential customers may be facing. It would seem ridiculous for an entrepreneur to spend time and energy convincing a potential client that they don't have a serious problem and only need a slight "tweak". If a salesman approaches consumers with that mindset, a sale is unlikely and he would eventually be out of business.

Any one of Trump's rivals could have adopted the same goal of making America great and built a campaign around this concept. As a bi-partisan, widely inclusive goal, it resonates with demographics across the board. By being "first out of the gate" Trump was able to position himself well and gain an impressive edge over the competition.

Strategy #5 – Dominate Social Media!

The strategic use of media and advertising has long been one of the foundational pillars of a successful business. As technology has improved and changed through the years, so have the methods of creating excitement around a product or service and ultimately boost sales. Whether through the newspaper, radio, television, billboards, Internet, or word of mouth, businesses will do well if they can communicate successfully with a relevant consumer base. The political realm is no exception; candidates who can get their message out and interact with voters, supporters, and critics will be much more successful in their run for office.

"If you can put politics aside, there are many social media lessons to learn from the Donald Trump presidential campaign. His

team, and the Republican nominee himself, have used social media as a way to garner media attention in ways that are worth noting for any brand."

~ Mary C. Long, Business.com

Departure from Television Advertising

In the past, the main method of getting the word out and convincing people to vote for a certain candidate was through direct advertising. A candidate's success often hinged on how well he or she managed their method of advertising and whether or not they had sufficient funding to support their endeavors. This type of advertising could cost millions of dollars, which has historically meant that politicians faced a built-in financial barrier when trying to win an election.

In 1964, the success of Lyndon Johnson's presidential campaign was partially successful through his use of television ads, considered at the time to be an innovative tool. Watching television was a novelty and an important part of socializing. With mainstream voters watching television every night, a candidate's message could be easily conveyed. During both of his successful bids for the presidency, Barack Obama went beyond television ads to incorporate social media and various technologies to reach his voters.

Since 1952, this political season may mark the beginning of an era where television is relatively unimportant. No longer the most effective way to publicize a political campaign to potential voters, Trump's rivals have continued to use television ads to a large degree. Perhaps due to his business background, Trump seemed to realize this fact early on. While his competitors may have been confused by his focus on social media over paid television ads, he has been able to manipulate the attention focused on him through both the strategies in Chapter 1 and his social media communication. Choosing to focus on free and inexpensive means of advertising almost exclusively has resulted in an equally competitive campaign against opponents who have spent billions of dollars advertising.

Twitter Marketing

This may be the first election cycle where candidates communicate with younger demographics like the Millennials and Gen Z via Facebook and Twitter. Once again, Trump has demonstrated his insight from the business world by his use of tools such as Twitter to get messages out to the right audience at the perfect time. In addition, simply by being present on Twitter, he has demonstrated to the younger generations he is in touch with technological trends and able to communicate with his audience using tools they are comfortable with. His use of tweets, along with various content have allowed him to advertise his political brand while appearing connected to younger generations. Consumers are increasingly demanding information that is concise, clear and frequent – which is exactly how Twitter is used. Being forced to condense a point to the standard 140 characters required by Twitter means candidates have no choice but to be clear with their messages. With no room for flowery phrasing and a demand for brevity, social media has actually worked well for Trump's brief and unfiltered style. Twitter and Facebook meet the demand for frequent and accessible information, and Trump's 10 tweets a day and a variety of Facebook posts have positioned him as a front-runner in this regard.

Facebook and Internet Marketing

Internet marketing creates significant opportunity for getting a sales pitch to the audience it needs to reach while also communicating with supporters. Whether you are selling a product, a service, or a political agenda, incorporating technology is an essential part of the game in both business and politics. In the marketing realm, each touch point needs to inspire the consumer to take action; in the political world, a voter. Whether the messages are getting to potential voters through candidate websites, microsites, online ads or email campaigns, communication must be relevant and compelling.

Similar to other aspects of his political campaign strategy, Donald Trump has excelled at marketing himself as a viable candidate through his social media efforts. Since the early part of his campaign, one of his best communication channels has been

Facebook. Not only has Trump strategically used Facebook to reach a large segment of his target market, but he also became active on social media before his competitors even caught on. After announcing his desire to run for presidency, both his competitors were caught off guard. No one was prepared for the clamor that resulted from his announcement, and he was able to leverage this rush of attention to bolster his presence on social media. Posting clear, concise messages to his Facebook page, Trump has followed the same principle his mission statement does: to be easily understood. With every post connecting to his campaign theme, he has truly "trumped" his rivals on social media, maintaining a greater amount of "likes" and followers than any of his competitors.

> *"I have made the tough decisions, always with an eye toward the bottom line. Perhaps it's time America was run like a business."*
>
> *~ Donald Trump*

By differentiating his political brand from the competition even on Facebook, Trump has gained a large amount of support by positioning himself as an outsider, impervious to the influence of a corrupt political system. Trump has gained a lot of leverage from reaffirming his image as being everything his rivals are not. Portraying himself as a businessman with the skills and experience to fix what is wrong with America, he constantly reiterates his disregard for the status quo and his distain for the underlying agendas of the present-day powers. At first glance, viewers can immediately see his Facebook page is different. While most official political pages invite visitors to "sign up" by clicking a button that links to their official website, Trump's page doesn't have a "sign up" button. Instead, he has a "shop now" button that leads directly to merchandise for his political brand. Of course, the retail page is part of his informational campaign website, but the button on his Facebook page links to a store rather than the traditional campaign page. As any great marketer would do, Trump ensures he is noticeably different from the competition, and his "shop now" button may seem like a small detail, but it allows him to stand out as a successful businessman rather than a traditional politician. For voters who are frustrated with ongoing corruption and hold a deep mistrust of the political system, it offers a refreshing change.

Promotional Products

Another intriguing strategy Trump has employed is his use of campaign merchandise to advertise and generate brand loyalty. Whether it's a "Make America Great Again" cap, a Trump/Pence t-shirt, or a sticker on a vehicle, voters literally become walking billboards, using Trump's campaign products in their everyday lives. While candidates running for political office are prohibited from receiving any personal profits from the sale of campaign merchandise, they are permitted to use the profits for campaign expenses such as advertisements, venue rentals or signage. Affordable prices set on his campaign merchandise show he understands that putting the merchandise in the hands of as many people as possible greatly outweighs the financial gain that could be accomplished by pricing higher.

Consistency and the Personal Touch through Digital Communications

Whether it's through social networks, email, or his website, every communication going out seems to come directly from Donald Trump himself. While he may very likely have staff that post for him, his clear tone and authentic voice is evident in each and every message. A savvy marketer has mastered the art of crafting their messaging to speak directly to their audience, addressing the exact problems they are facing, and Trump's business background becomes evident in his ability to accomplish this.

Overall, Trump's strategic use of social media to market his brand is one of the most powerful campaign tools in his arsenal. Marketers and politicians alike can take notes from the way Trump has communicated with his fans, supporters, undecided voters, and even his most fervent adversaries through simple and inexpensive social methods. To succeed politically, a candidate requires either sound financial management or unlimited resources, and Trump's business and marketing skills have demonstrated that when social media is used creatively in a cost-effective way, a lot can be accomplished.

> *"The Trump story is a case study that should inspire a renewed faith in content marketing and social media over traditional channels of communications. But it should also provide a reminder that these tools work best when the product is a person and that person happens to be naturally, horrendously, enduringly fascinating."*
> *~ Mark Ritson, Branding Strategy Insider*

Conclusion

Congratulations and thank you again for purchasing this book and reading it all the way to this point!

This book is not about politic, but rather it is more like a business case study of a businessman who entered the political world. I hope you have enjoyed reading this book, and have learned something valuable from it.

Finally, if you enjoyed this book, then I'd like to ask you for a favor, would you be kind enough to leave a review for this book on Amazon? Tell us what you like or dislike and what we can improve. Your feedbacks will be greatly appreciated!

https://www.amazon.com/dp/B01LRLIT7G

Also follow EntrepreneurshipFacts on social media to stay updated with our new books and increase your knowledge about business and successful people on a daily basis:

Instagram　　　　Facebook　　　　Twitter

Check out our website for the latest facts and articles about business and entrepreneurship:

www.EntrepreneurshipFacts.com

More books by Entrepreneurship Facts

101 Entrepreneurial Facts About 10 of The Most Successful BILLIONAIRES That Can Inspire You: What you can learn from their successes

The Real Life RICH DAD & The Lessons He Taught ROBERT KIYOSAKI about Money

Warren Buffett - 41 Fascinating Facts about Life & Investing Philosophy: The Lessons From A Legendary Investor

Elon Musk - Top 10 Business Lessons Through An Inspiring Life Of A Visionary Entrepreneur:

10 Most Outrageous Donald Trump Quotes

1. "I will build a great wall – and nobody builds walls better than me, believe me – and I'll build them very inexpensively. I will build a great, great wall on our southern border, and I will make Mexico pay for that wall. Mark my words."

2. "When Mexico sends its people, they're not sending the best. They're not sending you, they're sending people that have lots of problems and they're bringing those problems with us. They're bringing drugs. They're bring crime. They're rapists... And some, I assume, are good people."

3. "Our great African-American President hasn't exactly had a positive impact on the

thugs who are so happily and openly destroying Baltimore."

4. "All of the women on The Apprentice flirted with me – consciously or unconsciously. That's to be expected."

5. "The beauty of me is that I'm very rich."

6. "It's freezing and snowing in New York – we need global warming!"

7. "I think the only difference between me and the other candidates is that I'm more honest and my women are more beautiful."

8. "My IQ is one of the highest — and you all know it! Please don't feel so stupid or insecure; it's not your fault."

9. "The only card [Hillary Clinton] has is the woman's card. She's got nothing else to offer and frankly, if Hillary Clinton were a man, I don't think she'd get 5 percent of the vote. The only thing she's got going is the woman's card, and the beautiful thing is, women don't like her."

10. "If Hillary Clinton can't satisfy her husband what makes her think she can satisfy America?"

www.ingramcontent.com/pod-product-compliance
Lightning Source LLC
Chambersburg PA
CBHW060400190526
45169CB00002B/682